Words & Music
Chris While and Julie Matthews

Published by Circuit Music Limited

Acknowledgments

Special thanks go to the following people.
Bryan Ledgard, our graphic designer and friend who always comes up with the goods.
Chris Euesden, our publishing partner, friend and constant supporter.
Eric, Kristina and **Judy**, for their kind words.
Joe While for the beautiful and carefully hand written manuscripts and for the many hours
of transcribing the music from our CDs.
Helen Watson, our co-writer on 'Hard to be the Way' and an inspiration to us always.
Jil Barke, not only for being our best friend but for keeping the whole thing
going so smoothly and efficiently.

All the people who sing our songs, from those we don't know about to those we do –
**Mary Black, Frances Black, Barbara Dickson, Kathy Chiavola, Fairport Convention,
John Wright, Mary Duff, Christine Collister, Kellie While** and **Iona** and **Andy**.
Apologies to those not mentioned; your performance is no less appreciated but our memories fail us!

To the following, we give our love;
Mum, Dad, Susan, Danny, Laura, Kellie, Kwame, Callie, Steve B. and **Marvin**.

This book is copyright under the Berne Convention. All rights are reserved.
Apart from any fair dealing for the purpose of private study, research, criticism or review, as permitted under
the Copyright, Designs and Patents Act 1988, no part of this publication may be reproduced, stored in a
retrieval system, or transmitted in any form or by any means, electronic, electrical, chemical, mechanical,
optical, photocopying, recording or otherwise, without the prior written permission of the copyright owner.
Enquiries should be addressed to Circuit Music Ltd.

ISBN 0-9543256-0-5
ISMN M 9002067 0 1

First published 2002

Published by Circuit Music Ltd., 1 Holly Terrace, York YO10 4DS
Telephone 01904 610899
www.circuitfatcat.co.uk

All songs are published by Circuit Music Ltd.,
except for *Hard To Be The Way* © Circuit Music Ltd./Sanctuary Music Publishing Ltd.
Sanctuary Music Publishing Ltd., Sanctuary House, 45-53 Sinclair Road, London W14 0NS

Designed in England by Ledgard Jepson Limited
Printed in England by The Nuffied Press Limited

"I wish I'd written that"

– now there's a wistful little phrase that every songwriter is all too familiar with. Half-envious and half-admiring, you mutter it to yourself with varying degrees of frequency when listening to the songs of other songwriters, the frequency usually being dictated by the musical talent and expertise of the songwriter in question, and also by how many more painful personal admissions of musical inadequacy your already battered ego can withstand.

When listening to the songs of Chris While and Julie Matthews however, the muttering of this wistful little phrase increases from varying degrees of frequency to an almost incessant litany. They are very good songwriters indeed. As a fellow songwriter, and therefore I suppose in some ways a competitor, I have the choice of either admitting this fact through gritted teeth or open-mouthed, slack-jawed admiration. You can put me in the slack-jawed category, with perhaps a slight hint of a background grinding of teeth! I am an unashamed fan of their songwriting talents, I admit it, I'll come clean, I am not an unbiased observer. Which is not all that surprising an admission I suppose, Chris and Julie would hardly get someone who hated their songs to write an introduction to them.

Chris and Julie's songs are not mawkish manufactured schlock written with one hand on the rhyming dictionary and eyes fixed firmly on the pop charts. They are real, human songs, written with, and containing lots of, heart and humour, passion and compassion, insight and simplicity, honesty and directness. They are in fact an accurate reflection of the attitudes and personalities of their composers, and that, in no small measure, is why they are so damned good.

And it's the quality of their songs that will sell this book, not any words of mine, although it has been a pleasure and a privilege to make this small contribution. Finally, a word of warning. This songbook contains songs that may well attempt to stir your heart. Do not be alarmed. Just relax and remember, to quote from one of Julie's songs (Not included in this book – why, Julie, why? It's one of my faves):

> The heart holds your best intuition
> So follow it into the darkness and out to the light
> Who knows? – the heart may be right"

I wish I'd written that ...

Eric Bogle

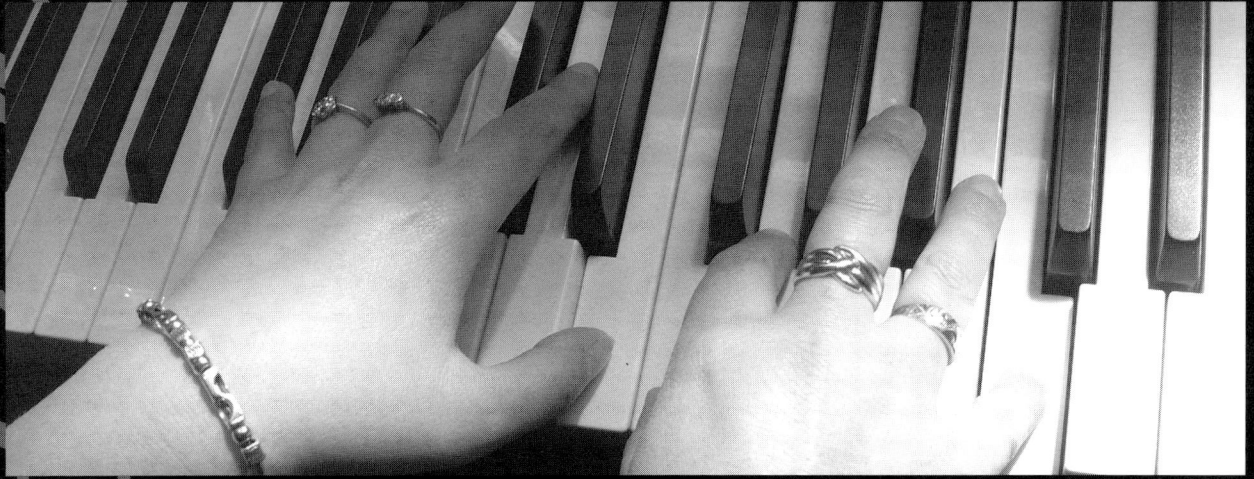

Contents

100 Miles

Chris While © Circuit Music

Featured on the albums *Still on Fire/By Request*, *Look At Me Now* and *Stages*

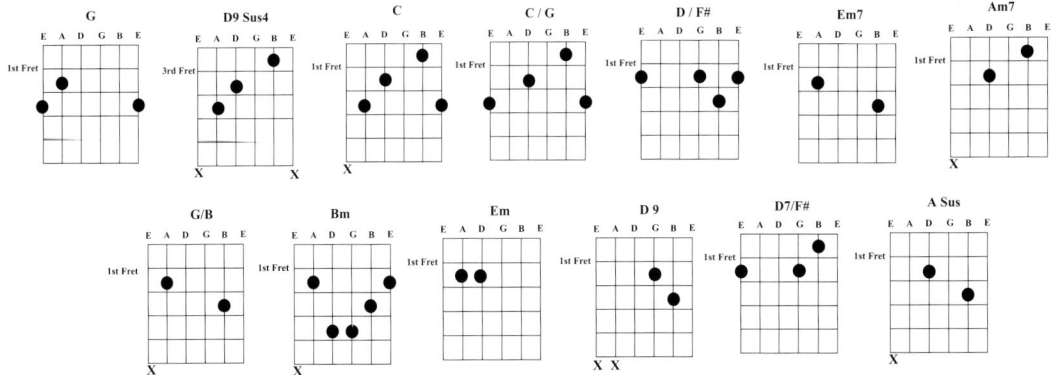

It's on-ly hours since I was with you But ev-en so it seems
like years So ma-ny words un-said be-tween us
hang in the air like sou — ven-irs I have so much I want
to tell you But I am scared to push that far
Could I reach out my heart and touch you —— And find out
who you real-ly are
But there's a hun-dred miles be-tween —— us And I can
feel your breath in my hair Oh when the wind blows and I'm
blown home — ward I long to see you stand-ing there
Last line
I long to see you stand-ing there ——

100 Miles

Chris While © Circuit Music

It's only hours since I was with you
But even so it seems like years
So many words unsaid between us
Hang in the air like souvenirs

I have so much I want to tell you
But I am scared to push that far
Could I reach out my heart and touch you
And find out who you really are

Chorus
But there's a hundred miles between us
And I can feel your breath in my hair
Oh! When the wind turns and I'm blown homeward
I long to see you standing there

The road winds on into the distance
The view behind me fades away
It won't be long before I see you
I have to get through just one more day

And I see your face in every window
I read your name on every sign
I hear your voice when the wind blows through me
And I feel your presence all the time

Chorus

I long to see you standing there

*In 1991 some friends and I spent a week in a beach house in Nefyn, Wales.
I wrote a number of songs in this beautiful place, this is my 'missing you song'.*

Albion Heart

Matthews and While © Circuit Music

Featured on the album *Albion Heart* (Albion Band)

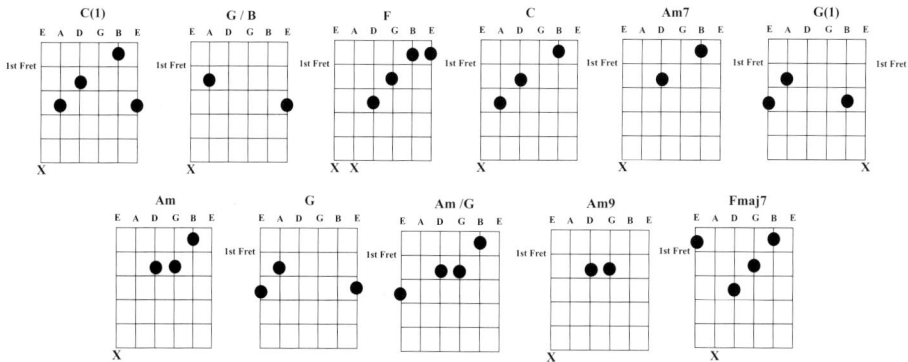

C(1) G / B F C Am7 G(1)

Am G Am /G Am9 Fmaj7

These are the chord shapes we use with the capo on the third fret.

[G/B] Hard times made a [F] gyp-sy of [C] him

[G/B] Carried a-way on an em-i-grant [F] wind [C] Be-

[Am7] hind him the white cliffs were fad-ing a-way The [F] un-known hor-i-[C] zon was

[G] call-ing [C(1)] With tears in his eyes he [F] said his good-byes [Am7] to

[G/B] Eng-land

[G/B] Good-bye to my [C] home-land — [F] Now [G] we're a-[Am7] part [Am/G] — [Fmaj7] I'll

[C] keep you in mind Ne-ver [G] leave you be-hind in my [C] Al-bi-on heart

Albion Heart

Matthews and While © Circuit Music

Hard times made a gypsy of him
Carried away on an emigrant wind
Behind him the white cliffs were fading away
The unknown horizon was calling
With tears in his eyes he said his goodbyes to England

Chorus
So goodbye to my homeland
Now we're apart
I'll keep you in mind, never leave you behind
In my Albion heart

She was born of higher degree
And their love was shared secretly
In separate circles condemned by his class
He left for America's shore
Vowing to come back a gentleman one day to England

Chorus

After seven long years the wind turned around
And a gentleman now for England was bound
No longer a tradesman he came to her door
With love in his heart overflowing
He swept her away, they married that day there in England

Chorus
So here in my homeland
We never will part
I kept you in mind, never left you behind
In my Albion heart

Chris and I were in Canada when we wrote this in our agent's basement. We followed the idea of the working class man leaving his beloved home in order to prove his worth and improve his standing with his high-class lover. It's a 'broken-token' song and as we were in the Albion Band at the time, Albion, being an old word for England seemed an appropriate title. For our remaining years with Albion Band, the song became something of an anthem, we are still asked for it now at gigs.

Angels Walk Among Us

Julie Matthews © Circuit Music

Featured on the albums *Higher Potential* and *Stages*

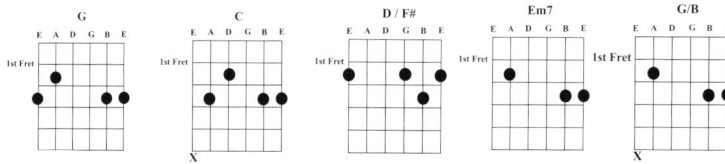

These are the chord shapes we use with the capo on the third fret.

[G] [Em7] [D/F#] [G/B] [C] [D/F#]
Do you re-mem-ber you were down on your luck you held your hand out to a stran-ger

[G] [Em7] [D/F#] [G/B] [C] [D/F#]
Some-thing in his eyes you al-most rec-og-nised some-thing in that look changed you

[C] [D/F#] [G/B] [C] [D/F#]
Brought you out of the mad-ness Some-how made you strong-er I be-

[G] [Em7] [C] [D/F#] [Em7] [C]
-lieve an-gels walk a-mong us I be-lieve an-

[D/F#] [G] [Em7] [G/B] [C]
-gels walk a-mong us I be-lieve I be-lieve an-

[D/F#] [G]
-gels walk a-mong us

[C] [G/B]
mong us We get so caught up in the small-er stuff

[C] [D/F#] [C] [Em7]
we miss the bigg-er pic-ture 'Til some-thing so pro-found knocks us down

[C] [D/F#] [Em7] [G/B]
and sudd-en-ly it hits you An-gels a-mong us

Angels Walk Among Us

Julie Matthews © Circuit Music

Do you remember you were down on your luck
You held your hand out to a stranger?
Something in his eyes
You almost recognised
Something in that look changed you
Took you out of the madness
Somehow made you stronger
I believe that angels walk among us

Chorus
I believe angels walk among us
I believe, I believe angels walk among us

All she remembers is she was falling
And the ground was getting nearer
"Oh God forgive me," she said, "please be with me
In this moment it all seems clearer"
With 20 feet left to fall, she stalled
And her skirt blew out around her
Set her down
Where angels walk among us

Chorus

We get so caught up in the smaller stuff
We miss the bigger picture
'Til something so profound knocks us down
And suddenly it hits you
Angels among us

It's in the eyes of the sleeping child
And the mother's look of wonder
It's in the arms of the one I love
And the magic spell I'm under
It's in the feeling there's someone here
When I'm sitting on my own
I'm not alone, 'cause angels walk among us

Chorus

I picked up a leaflet put out by the Bristol tourist board to counteract the terrible history that the Clifton Suspension Bridge has as having the highest suicide rate for any one place in Britain. It wrote of a young girl at the turn of the last century who threw herself off the bridge but was saved by her petticoat acting like a parachute and breaking her fall. She went on to live a long and happy life, leading me to the idea that maybe some things that happen in our lives are led by 'forces' outside ourselves or our own influence. I like to call these angels.

Another Year Another Day

Chris While © Circuit Music

Featured on the albums *Still on Fire* and *Daphne's Flight*

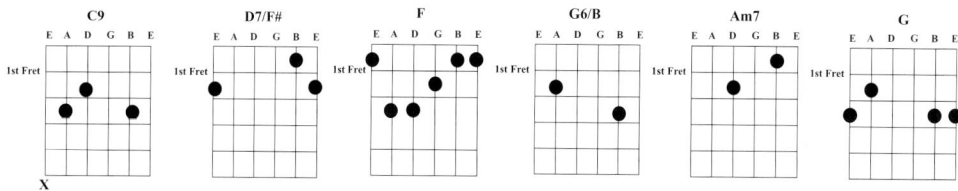

(You Know) Pain is a bitter pill to swal-low when your life seems so arr-anged And you're
blind to what's been happ-en-ing in front of your eyes And you don't see on-y-thing strange And
pride is a long long fall when the ground be-neath your feet is strong You don't
plan for it to crumb-le You don't plan for it to fall though your patience and past is so long
How could you treat me like this How could you use me so
May-be in a-no-ther year in a-no-ther hour on a-no-ther day May-be I'll let
go
There may be good times round the cor-ner Ah but I can't see that far yet There's just a
tap-es-try of pain-ful me-mo-ries That'll nev-er nev-er for - get

last line

May-be I've let go — May-be I've let go — May-be I've let go

Another Year Another Day

Chris While © Circuit Music

You know pain is bitter pill to swallow
When your life seems so arranged
And you're blind to what's been happening –
in front of your eyes
And you don't feel anything strange
Pride is a long, long fall
When the ground beneath your feet is strong
And you don't plan for it to crumble
You don't plan for it to fall
Though your patience and past is so long

Chorus
How could you treat me like this
How could you use me so
Maybe in another year, in another hour, on another day
Maybe I'll let go

And blind is a bad, bad place
When your eyes are searching so hard
And you're hoping that you'll see it in the back of his eyes
And it was there all the time in your back yard

Chorus

There may be good times round the corner
But I can't see that far yet
There's just a tapestry of painful memories
That I'll never, never forget

Chorus x 2

Baby I'll let go
Baby I'll let go
Maybe I've let go
Baby, baby, baby I've let go
Baby, baby, baby I've let go

After years of being a singer and not a writer of songs, this was the first song to emerge after my 17 year marriage ended in 1991. It was first recorded on 'Still on Fire' and it later surfaced again on the Daphne's Flight Album.

Blue Moon On The Rise

Matthews and While © Circuit Music

Featured on the extended single *Blue Moon On The Rise*

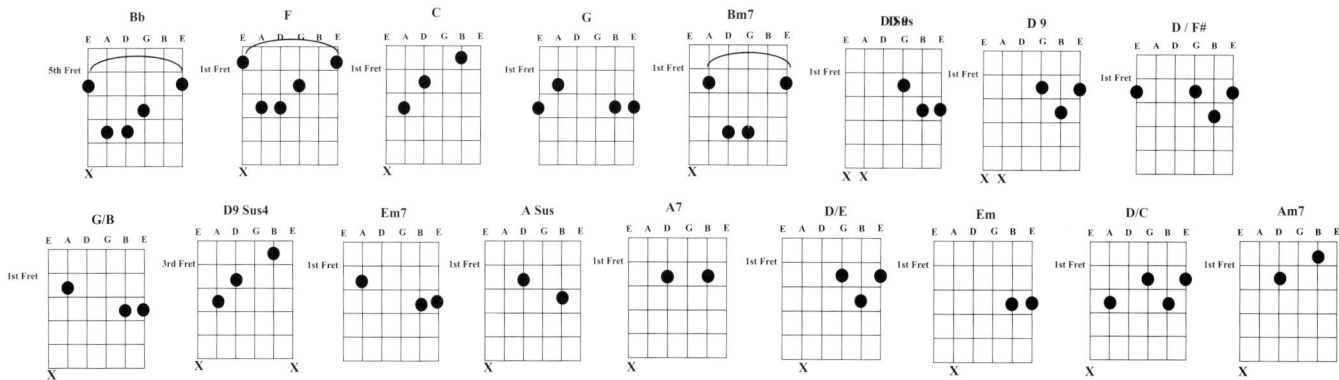

Blue Moon On The Rise

Matthews and While © Circuit Music

All along the beaches, the big ships are leaving
You're tied to the edge of the sea
You've watched them come and go
And how your heart reaches
Oh how you long to be free
But in a careless moment
You were blinded by love
No more than a baby yourself
And now the young girl cries for the baby inside
He doesn't want to hear it and she'll never tell, so

Chorus
Hold tight your childish notion
A dream that never dies
You're anchored here by the ocean
Blue moon on the rise

Wind blows, a child grows
Small steps, love flows
Between the woman and the child
And the child in the woman never goes, and it shows
It still shows

All along the beaches, the big ships are leaving
You're tied to the edge of the sea.
You've watched them come and go
And she's watched them with you
Your baby she was born to be free
Then in a selfless moment, guided by love
You gave her wings to fly
And as she pulled away from the edge of the sea
The blue moon turned gold in your eye so

Chorus
Hold tight your childish notion
A dream that never dies
Love's anchored here near the ocean
Blue moon on the rise
Blue moon on the rise

1994 – This is the first co-write for Julie and I. Recorded on our CD single of the same name.

Blue Songs On A Red Guitar

Julie Matthews © Circuit Music

Featured on the albums *Such Is Life*, *Still on Fire/By Request* and *Stages*

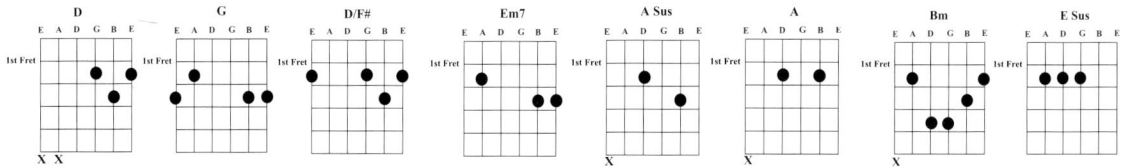

D   G   D/F#   Em7   A Sus   A   Bm   E Sus

[D] Me and my sha-dow were ne-ver a-[A]part [G] We know the bl-[D/F#] [Em7] [D/F#]

ves by [Asus] heart Sing them in the mor-ning with the s-[D] [A] [G]

un on the [D/F#] rise Sing them at [Em7] night [D/F#] to star studd-ed [Em] skies [A] And

[G] I'm not cra-zy [D/F#] though it looks that [Em] way It's just [G] that [D/F#] m-

e and my sha-dow like to [Esus] [Asus] play

[D] Blue songs on [A] a red gui-[G] tar [D] Me and my [G] sha-[D/F#]

dow do a fine rou-[Esus] tine [Asus] And it's tak-ing the ach-[D/F#] ing [A] right

[Bm] out of my [Esus] heart Play-ing [Em7] blues on a [Asus] red gui-tar

[G] And I will not be de-[Bm] nied my sorr-ow I've earned the ri-[Em7]

[G] ght to feel this [D] way May-be [G] I will change my tune to-morr-[Bm]

[Esus] ow But just to-night I'll think I'll [Asus] play

Blue Songs On A Red Guitar

Julie Matthews © Circuit Music

Me and my shadow we're never apart
We know the blues by heart
We sing them in the morning with the sun on the rise
Sing them at night to star studded skies
And I'm not crazy though it looks that way
It's just that me and my shadow like to play

Chorus
Blue songs on a red guitar
Me and my shadow do a fine routine
And it's taking the aching right out of my heart
Playing blues on a red guitar

Well I talk to the walls but the walls never hear
My pillow won't dry up none of my tears
But when the night comes down and my shadow comes out
She knows what all of this heartache's about
And I'm not afraid of the darkness you see
It's only my shadow that's following me....singing

Chorus

And I will not be denied my sorrow
I've earned the right to feel this way
Maybe I will change my tune tomorrow
But just tonight I think I'll play

Chorus

Taking the aching right out of my heart
Playing blues on a red guitar

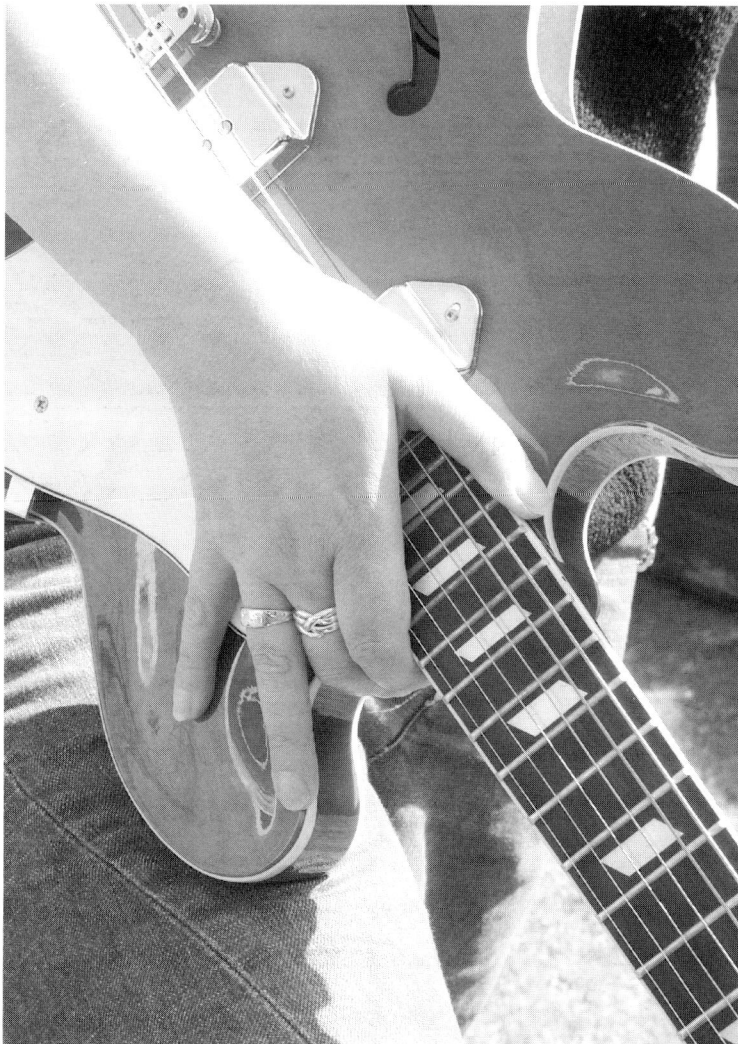

This title was with me for a year or so before I wrote the song and yes I really did have a red guitar!

Can't Get The Wares Away

Matthews and While © Circuit Music

Featured on the album *Heart Of England*

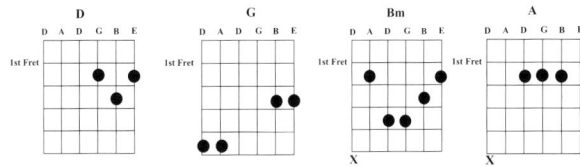

This song uses a dropped D. To do this, tune your bottom E string down to D.

Can't Get The Wares Away

Matthews and While © Circuit Music

Well we spin and weave from morn 'til night
But we can't get the wares away
And the foundry flare is a constant sight
But we can't get the wares away

Well we make it fast and we make it good
But we can't get the wares away
Now it's piling up like firewood
'Cause we can't get the wares away

Chorus
Oh we can't get the wares away
We can't get the wares away
To the ships in Liverpool bay
Oh! We can't get the wares away

Well the foundry hammer will soon be still
'Cause we can't get the wares away
And the gates will close on the cotton mill
If we can't get the wares away

Well we need a way and we need it fast
'Cause we can't get the wares away
Or these industries will never last
If we can't get the wares away

Chorus x 2

We were commissioned by the BBC to write the music for a radio documentary on the building of the Manchester Ship Canal. It was a really interesting project to do, with lots of research given to us at the start. This is one of the songs that came out of it and has been in and out of our live set ever since.

Circle Round The Sun

Chris While © Circuit Music

Featured on the albums *Daphne's Flight* and *Stages*

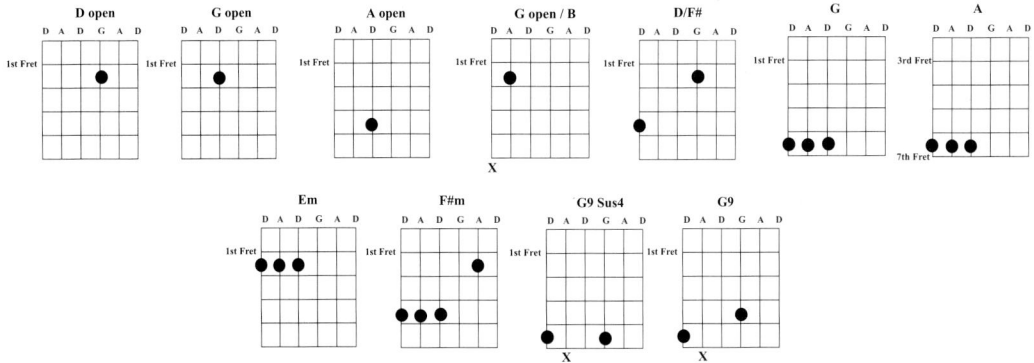

This song uses a DADGAD tuning. Once you have tuned the strings, these are the shapes you will need.

[D] Eve-ry-bo-dy says that love is [G] just a-round the cor-ner [D] And

[A] peace is just a-no-ther state of heart And

[D] fate could be a dif-fer-ent way of [G] simp-ly stopp-ing try-ing [D] And

death is just a [A] place for us to [D] start One

[G/B] batt-le may-be o — ver one more may be in [D/F#] sight And we

[G] put off till to-mor-row [F#m] what we [Em] fear to do to-[A]night And we

[D] fight un-til we're bro-ken And we [G9sus] live un-til we [G9] fall Al-ways

[D] turn-ing for-ev-er [A] twin-ing And we [D] circ-le [G] round the [A] sun

And we [D] circ-le [G] round the [A] sun And we [D] circ-le [G] round the

[A] sun un-til we're [D] done

Circle Round The Sun

Chris While © Circuit Music

Everybody says that love is just around the corner and peace is just another state of heart
And fate could be a different way of simply stopping trying and death is just a place for us to start
One battle may be over, one more may be in sight and we put off till tomorrow what we fear to do tonight
And we fight until we're broken and we love until we fall, always turning, forever turning

Chorus
And we circle round the sun
And we circle round the sun
And we circle round the sun
Until we're done.

And we cast a longing eye to the grass that's always greener and march to take the land that's greener still
And we follow one who's stronger even when we don't agree and struggle to conform against our will
We brave the nine to five to pay for mortgages and cars and we spend an earthly fortune to fly a man to Mars
But we laugh until we cry and we cry ourselves to sleep, always turning, forever turning
Chorus

So the human race moves forward, destination God knows where, while the planet slowly spins the hands of time
And we long for inner peace, while we search for outer space and undiscovered mountains still to climb.
The starving pray in circles for the sky to bring them rain, we watch them via satellites and turn our heads in shame
And we yearn the new beginnings while we dread the final end, always turning, forever turning

Chorus

This song was written for an album called 'Demi-Paradise' by the Albion Band (of which we were members).
We also recorded it on 'Daphne's Flight' and later on our live album 'Stages'. It has since been recorded by other people
around the world but remains something of an anthem for the duo.

Class Reunion

Julie Matthews © Circuit Music

Featured on the albums *Piecework* and *Stages*

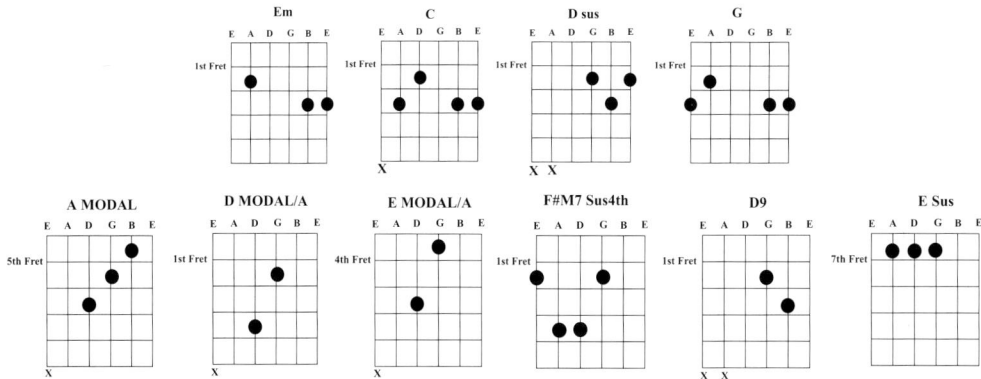

These are the chord shapes we use with the capo on the second fret.

1. [Em] Mon-day morn-ing when the pa-pers came The ad jumped out on the [C] pers-on-al page

2. [Em] Were you in the class of [C] sev-en-ty eight [Dsus] If so let's [C] make a date

3. [Esus] Make a date for a class re-un-ion All re-plies please send to [G] Su-san [C] Lt

4. [Esus] all come back like the worst of dreams Su-san was the cap-tain of the net-ball team

5. [Em] na na na [C] na na na [Dsus] na na na na na na [C] na na na

6. She was the i-dol of us then Stood like an Am-a-zon at five feet ten

7. Girls and boys a-like a-dored her My ve-ry pre-sence bored her

8. So I found my-self a-lone on the bus to school and the bus back home

9. On the out-side of the ring ad-o-lesc-ent pain is a deep deep thing

Verses 1 and 2: lines 1 to 4 then chorus line 5.

Verse 3: lines 6 to 9 then chorus line in B Major (guitar use modal chords)

Verses 4 and 5: lines 1 to 4 in B Major (guitar use modal chords)

Class Reunion

Julie Matthews © Circuit Music

Monday morning when the papers came,
The ad jumped out on the personal page
Were you in the class of '78, if so let's make a date
Make a date for a class reunion
All replies please send to Susan
It all came back like the worst of dreams
Susan was the captain of the netball team

It all came back in a cloak of hurt
Standing in line in my netball skirt
The names were called out one by one
Mine wasn't picked it was forced upon
Susan Collins and her glorious team
But I was the weak link in between
I can't throw and I can't catch
Enough to say we lost the match

Na na na na na na ...

She was the idol of us then
Stood like an Amazon five feet ten
Girls and boys alike adored her
My very presence bored her
So I found myself alone
On the bus to school and the bus back home
On the outside of the ring
Adolescent pain is a deep, deep thing

Na na na na na na ...

Well God knows how I found the nerve
But I pulled my car up to the kerb
The kerb outside the entrance hall
The school hadn't changed that much at all
Fifteen years of hurt lay buried
A moment like this can't be hurried
I sat frozen in my seat
When a car pulled up across the street

She looked up and caught my eye
Caught her breath in her surprise
And when She finally turned her gaze
I saw shame upon her face
Seems I'm not the only one
Haunted by the things she's done
I never went to the class reunion
I got drunk that night with Susan

Na na na na na na ...

Another story song, completely fictitious with an element of ... !
The song revolves around the Na-na chorus of the netball team, no matter where I took the story,
it always had to come back to that and I think that's what makes the song so successful live.

Even The Desert Bears A Seed

Matthews and While © Circuit Music

Featured on the albums *Piecework* and *Stages*

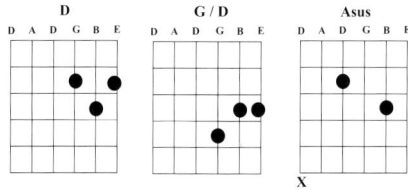

These chords are played on the 5th fret with bottom E dropped to D. We do use different bass notes sometimes but these are personal taste and change each time we play the song!

[D] [G/D] [Asus] [D]
May-be the things we wish for

[G/D] [Asus] [D]
Are not the things we need (but)

[G/D] [Asus] [D]
What we need is what we're gi-ven

[G/D] [Asus] [D]
Ev-en the des-ert bears a seed

[D] [G/D] [Asus] [D]
I wish she said for beau-ty

[G/D] [Asus] [D]
For looks to turn his head (but)

[G/D] [Asus] [D]
What the mirr-or does not show her

[G/D] [Asus] [D]
lies in her heart in-stead

[D] [G/D] [Asus] [D]
We spend our whole lives wish-ing

[G/D] [Asus] [D]
We search for eve-ry clue

[G/D] [Asus] [D]
We should look a litt-le clo-ser

[G/D] [Asus] [D]
For when we least ex-pect it

[G/D] [Asus] [D]
May-be it's what we're gi-ven

[G/D] [Asus] [D]
that will come shin-ing through

[D] [G/D] [Asus] [D]
Ev-en the des-ert bears a seed

[G/D] [Asus] [D]
Ev-en the des-ert bears a seed

Even The Desert Bears A Seed

Matthews and While © Circuit Music

Chorus
Maybe the things we wish for
Are not the things we need
But what we need is what we're given
Even the desert bears a seed

I wish she said for beauty, for looks to turn his head
But what the mirror does not show her
Lies in her heart instead

"I wish," he said, "for riches to buy her everything."
Although he may not know it, he is her rainbow's end

Chorus

We spend our whole lives wishing, we search for every clue
We should look a little closer for when we least expect it
Maybe it's what we're given that will come shining through

Chorus x 2

Even the desert bears a seed
Even the desert bears a seed

Often when we write together, the song starts with one of us having a riff, an idea or hook line. With 'Desert', I had written the chorus as my first venture on the mandolin, Chris then expanded the song with me. We actually completed the song in the car, on the M5 in a traffic jam - mandolins are useful for that!

Find My Way Back Home

Matthews and While © Circuit Music

Featured on the albums *Quest* and *Stages*

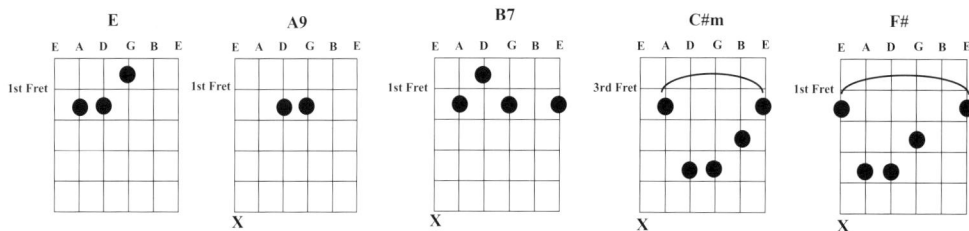

Find My Way Back Home

Matthews and While © Circuit Music

I'm gonna find my way back home
I'm gonna find my way back home
I'm gonna walk my feet down to the bone
I'm gonna find my way back home

Trouble leave your shoes untied
Trouble leave your shoes untied
'Cause you ain't coming on this ride
Trouble leave your shoes untied

Well the hungry wolf's been 'round my door
But now I'm going where the wolf ain't gonna
Howl no more

I've been sleeping underneath the moon
I've been sleeping underneath the moon
I'll be lying in my own bed soon
I've been sleeping underneath the moon

Well the hungry wolf's been 'round my door
But now I'm going where the wolf ain't gonna
Howl no more

I'm gonna find my way back home
I'm gonna find my way back home
I'm gonna walk my feet down to the bone
I'm gonna find my way back home
I'm gonna find my way back home

This was a fun and easy song to write. The repetitive lines in the verses were written with live audiences in mind and it was a good move, as the simplicity of it makes the audience feel they know the song instantly.

Hard To Be The Way

While, Matthews and Watson © Circuit Music/Sanctuary Music Publishing Ltd.

Featured on the albums *Piecework* and *Stages*

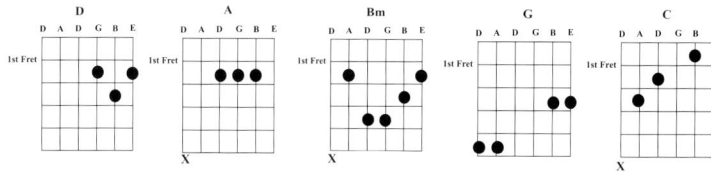

This song uses a dropped D. To do this, tune your bottom E string down to D.

Hard To Be The Way

While, Matthews and Watson © Circuit Music/Sanctuary Music Publishing

I can see you out there pacing the hall
Making something bigger out of something small
You don't want it without a price to pay
You just want hard to be the way

This should have blown over, you declared a war
You came in through the rubble darling
You could have used the door
You come out fighting with your eyes ablaze
You just want hard to be the way

Chorus
(Hard to be the way)
You could have made it easy but you'd rather have it
(Hard to be the way)
A torture and a torment simply out of habit
(Hard to be the way)
You just want hard to be the way

Is it easy for you, do you even know it
You can't help yourself, can't help but show it
It's the drama of it, it's the endless fight
You're attracted to it and it draws you in
Like a moth to the light
Hard to be the way

Chorus (without counter lines)

Chorus (with counter lines)

Roll up, roll up see the masochist at play, hey
You just want hard to be the way
You just want hard to be the way

Sitting in the garden in the summer of '96 we were playing music with our dear friend, the fantastic Helen Watson.
We had so much fun writing this together that we went on to write several more and I'm sure there'll be more to come!

I Can't Stay

Chris While © Circuit Music

Featured on the albums *Look At Me Now* and *Stages*

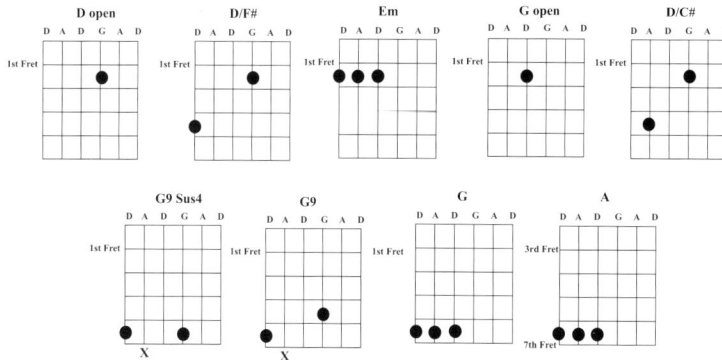

This song uses a DADGAD tuning. Once you have tuned the strings, these are the shapes you will need.

oh I [D] wish that I could call you [D/F#] or [Em] see [G] you eye to [D] eye

But I [D] know that if you come here [D/C#] I'll [Em] ne-ver say good-bye [G9sus] By the

[D] time you read this lett-er [D/F#] I'll be [G9] on my [G] way

If [D] you can't [Em] love me I [A] can't [D] stay

Last line repeat

If [D] you can't [Em] love me I [A] can't [D] stay

I Can't Stay

Chris While © Circuit Music

Oh I wish that I could call you or see you eye to eye
But I know that if you come here I'll never say goodbye
By the time you read this letter I'll be on my way
If you can't love me I can't stay

Well I reach the open doorway and take a last look at this place
And though burning tears they blind me, still I see your face
I recall your music playing and the sweet things you used to say
But if you can't love me I can't stay

What we shared was oh so special, so trusting and so true
But like the seasons ever changing I saw that change in you
Love was like a flowing river but now it's turned to clay
And if you can't love me I can't stay
If you can't love me I can't stay

Inspired by the film 'Now Voyager', a classic movie starring Bette Davis. I saw it when I was a teenager and have never forgotten it. I saw it again in 1991, went away and wrote this song.

Jewel In The Crown

Julie Matthews © Circuit Music

Featured on the albums *Such Is Life* and *Stages*

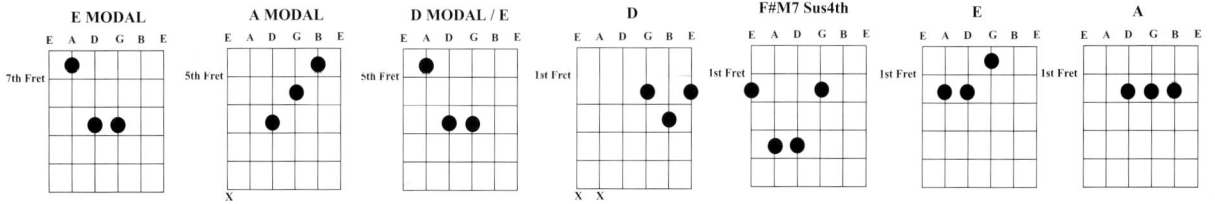

[Emod] We are a proud land We stand for free-dom We've got the fran-chise on how to lead them

[Amod] We've got the hist-ory and books to prove it Give us a moun-tain and we will move it

[Emod] We rule the waves and the sev-en seas We bring the might-y to their knees We

[Amod] off-er hope and ins-pi-ra-tion A fine ex-am-ple to less-er na-tions

[Emod] We are Bri-tann-ia [A] The jew-el in the crown

[A] We are Bri-[D]tann-ia We crowned an [F#M7] em-pire We came and [E] con-quered

[A] We tore their bor-ders down We need no [D] con-science God is on

[F#M7] our side We are Bri-[E]tann-ia The jew-el in the [A] crown

Jewel In The Crown

Julie Matthews © Circuit Music

We are a proud land we stand for freedom
We've got the franchise on how to lead them
We've got the history and books to prove it
Give us a mountain and we will move it
We rule the waves and the seven seas
We bring the mighty to their knees
We offer hope and inspiration
A fine example to lesser nations
We are Britannia the jewel in the crown

We brought a system to the masses
Divide the nation into classes
It's in our breeding and on our faces
At least we're all born knowing our places
We're raised within our social borders
We only take what our class affords us
It doesn't matter that it's not even
This is the nature of the demon
We are Britannia the jewel in the crown

We are Britannia, we crowned an empire
We came and conquered
We tore their borders down
We need no conscience
God is on our side
We are Britannia the jewel in the crown

We are your friendly liberators
We'll free your countries from their dictators
For a small slice of your oil wells
We'll send our boys in with their gun shells
We are an ally to the needy
We're always caring, never greedy
What other gesture could be kinder
We've given Hong Kong back to China
We are Britannia the jewel in the Crown

We are Britannia, we crowned an empire
We came and conquered
We tore their borders down
We need no conscience
God is on our side
We are Britannia the jewel in the crown
We are Britannia the jewel in the crown

I've been accused of being unpatriotic with this song.
I see it as a simple observation of my country's faults in both past and recent history.
It was recorded by Fairport Convention on their album of the same name.

Memories of You

Chris While © Circuit Music

Featured on the album *Still on Fire/By Request*

Well I've been sitt-ing here all day at the edge of the sea And I've

watched the sun roll down all the way from the east Well I've

picked at my gui-tar And I've picked at a lit-tle food But

most-ly I've been flick-ing through some mem-o-ries of you

You al-ways smiled when times were tough Your arms were wide when the ride was rou-

gh I think I'll stay here for a while Mem-o-ries of you make me smile

Memories of You

Chris While © Circuit Music

Well I've been sitting here all day at the edge of the sea
And I've watched the sun roll down all the way from the east
Well I've picked at my guitar and I've picked at a little food
But mostly I've been flicking through some memories of you

Chorus
You always smiled when times were tough, your arms were wide when the ride was rough
I think I'll stay here for a while, 'cause memories of you make me smile

Well I've been walking down familiar streets, same old faces I've chanced to meet
You walked me miles when I was a child and your time was always mine
Your hazel eyes were soft and kind, a family man with a family mind
Only one woman in your life, a loving mother, devoted wife
Chorus

I close my eyes I see your face and I'm in another time and place
When I felt I could do anything, we came alive when we heard you sing
But you've been gone for many years and I'm smiling now – look no tears
We never left a word unsaid, so simple was the life we led

Chorus

Memories of you make me smile

I was sitting on the beach one day in my home town of Barrow-in-Furness. Whilst watching the waves break I had a vivid memory of my Dad, Ben, carrying me over the pebbles (which hurt my feet) and into the sea. Then, with infinite patience, carried me back when I'd had enough. One memory leads to another...

Only One Man

Chris While © Circuit Music

Featured on the albums *Look At Me Now* and *Stages*

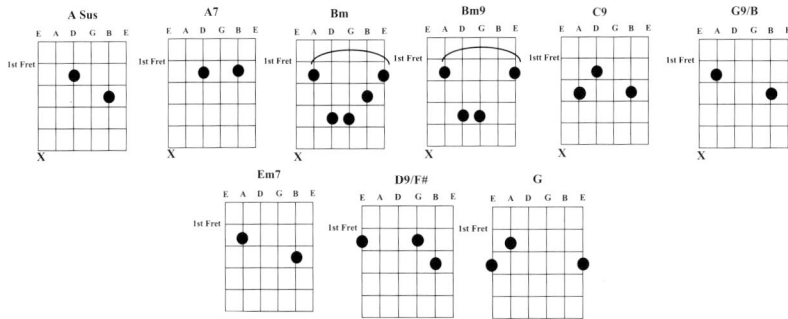

[Asus] [A7] [Asus] [A7]
I heard your voice for the first time last night After years of si-lence you said it right

[D9/F#] I'd been [Asus] [A7]
And all the words wait-ing for They're not im-por-tant an - y - more

[C9] [Em] [Asus]
I saw your eyes for the first time to-day Re-veal-ing truth in what you were say-ing

[D9/F#] [Asus] [A7]
And here I am at the edge of my seat I'm so scared I can't move my feet

[D9/F#] that's be- [G] [Bm7] [Asus]
Ne-ver scratch a wound gun to heal You're on-ly one man you're on-ly one man

[D9/F#] [G9/B] [Bm7] [Asus]
Leave it un-said don't tell me how you feel You're on-ly one man you're on-ly one man

[D9/F#] [G] [Em] [Asus]
Box it up keep the lid on tight You're on-ly one man you're on-ly one man And

[D9/F#] [G9/B] (slow) [Em] [Asus]
close the door as you turn out the light You're on-ly one

[Bm] [Bm9] [C9] [Bm]
man And I'm on-ly one wo-man

[C9] [Bm] [C9] [G9/B]
Feels like I've been wait- ing to see if you're love was true

[Em] [D9/F#] [G] [A7]
But I'm feel-ing the chan - ges in-to some-bo-dy new oh—

Only One Man

Chris While © Circuit Music

I heard your voice for the first time last night
After years of silence you said it right
And all the words I've been waiting for
They're not important anymore
I saw your eyes for the first time today
Revealing truth in what you were saying
And here I am on the edge of my seat
I'm so scared I can't move my feet

Chorus
Never scratch a wound that's begun to heal
You're only one man, you're only one man
Leave it unsaid don't tell me how you feel
You're only one man, you're only one man
Box it up keep the lid on tight
You're only one man, you're only one man
And close the door as you turn out the light
You're only one man, and I'm only one woman

You touched my face for the first time last night
I felt you tremble and I locked up tight
You only came 'cause she sent you away
And so you thought you'd ask me would I let you stay?
I saw right through you for the first time today
And I felt the fear start to fade away
I watched through curtains as you walked down the street
And I knew relief was gonna taste so sweet

Chorus

Seems like I've been waiting
To see if your love was true
But I've really been changing
Into somebody new

Oh baby, box it up keep the lid on tight
You're only one man, you're only one man
And close the door as you turn out the light
You're only one man, and I'm only one woman

After any break up there comes pain, anger, fear and eventually independence and liberty.
This is my 'finally letting go' song.

Piecework

Chris While © Circuit Music

Featured on the albums *Piecework* and *Stages*

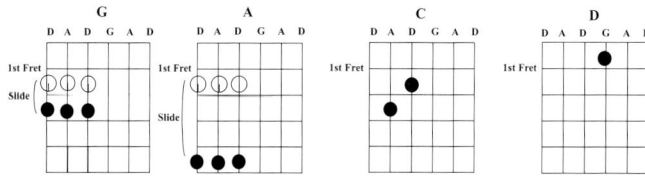

This song uses a DADGAD tuning. Once you have tuned the strings, these are the shapes you will need.

[D] I was on-ly fif-teen [G] when I came to this place With

[D] no-thing in my pock-et and a [G] smile on my face 'Cos there's this

[C] fine gui-tar in a [A] win-dow dis-[G] play And if

[G] I work hard she'll be [C] mine one [G] day

[D] Give me a twelve hour day I'm ne-ver gon-na shirk I'm sleep-in' like a ba-by when I'm [G]

[D] do-in' piece-work on [D] twelve hour days I'm ne-ver gon-na shirk I'm sleep-in' like a ba-by when I'm [C] [G]

[D] do-in' piece-work oh [D] piece-work [C] I'm do-in' piece-work [D]

[C] I've got bread in my lock-er I [G] heat the soup up in the can Keep-ing

[C] one eye on the clock and the [G] other on the man (hey)

page **40**

Piecework

Chris While © Circuit Music

I was only fifteen when I came to this place
With nothing in my pocket and a smile on my face
'Cause there's a fine guitar in a window display
And if I work hard she'll be mine one day

Chorus
Give me a twelve hour day, I'm never gonna shirk
I'm dreaming like a baby when I'm doing piecework
Oh twelve hour days, I'm never gonna shirk
I'm dreaming like a baby when I'm doing piecework
Oh piecework, I'm doing piecework

I've got forty-eight ends on the twisting line
I've tied a million knots in this two ply twine
And there's a foreman in blue who's always watching me
And it won't be long before he sees the back of me

Chorus

I've got bread in my locker, I heat the soup up in the can
Keeping one eye on the clock and the other on the man

Well, I saw blind Ron, he said I sing real good,
And I should leave this town before it dries my blood
He said he should've been gone twenty years ago
And now the shipyard's closing and he's got nowhere to go

Chorus x 2

Yeah, piecework, Oh I'm doing piecework

*I left school when I was fifteen and started work three days later in a wool factory called Listers.
My sister Susan worked on the spinning, my Mam on the packing, Dad was the joiner, Norman, my brother, worked nights
and my Grandad was the nightwatchman. I took my place in the twisting bay. As a budding musician, every hour
of piecework earned was spent on guitar payments and records.*

Shot Through The Heart

Julie Matthews © Circuit Music

Featured on the albums *Such Is Life* and *Stages*

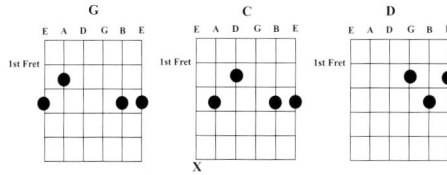

These are the chord shapes we use with the capo on the fifth fret.

She was a good girl   from a small town

Big ci-ty lights pulled her a- way

Ma-mma cried when she bought the tick-et

Da-ddy said it's a   sad sor-ry   day

Don't lis-ten to   a sweet-talk-er   with a dir-ty   mind

Don't dress like   a street-walk-er   You come from a diff-erent kind

Shot through the heart Shot through the heart   He had a strange ob-sess-ion

Shot through the heart Shot through the heart   She had a Smith and Wess-on

Shot Through The Heart

Julie Matthews © Circuit Music

She was a good girl from a small town
Big city lights pulled her away
Mama cried when she bought the ticket
Daddy said it's a sad sorry day
"Don't listen to a sweet talker with a dirty mind
Don't dress like a street walker
You come from a different kind"

He was bad blood, full of anger
Chip on his shoulder as big as a mountain
Like a time bomb, keep on ticking
Seconds passing but he ain't counting
He saw her at the station, such a perfect prize
With a fatal fascination, he watched with hungry eyes

Chorus
Shot through the heart, shot through the heart
He had a strange obsession
Shot through the heart, shot through the heart

She took a bus across the city
Found a motel that was cheap and clean
In the shadows on the sidewalk
He stood unnoticed and watched her checking in
She unpacked her belongings and placed on the shelf
The family photo and the pistol
That her Daddy had packed himself

Around midnight he took a side door
He climbed the stairway to the third floor
His heart pound at room twenty three
He used the switchblade like a pass-key
In the dark room,
He could just make out the bed and the figure
He touched the pillow, he felt the cold steel
She had her finger on the trigger

Chorus
Shot through the heart
Shot through the heart
He had a strange obsession
Shot through the heart
Shot through the heart
He had a strange obsession
Shot through the heart
Shot through the heart
He had a strange obsession
She had a Smith and Wesson
Shot through the heart

Chris calls this my 'Alfred Hitchcock' song! Story songs are great fun to write and a real challenge condensing the whole idea into 3-4 minutes and giving it just the right twist and punch at the end. I've been singing this live now for ten years and it still amazes me how audiences react to the last line.

Sister Moon

Chris While and Joe While © Circuit Music

Featured on the album *In The Big Room*

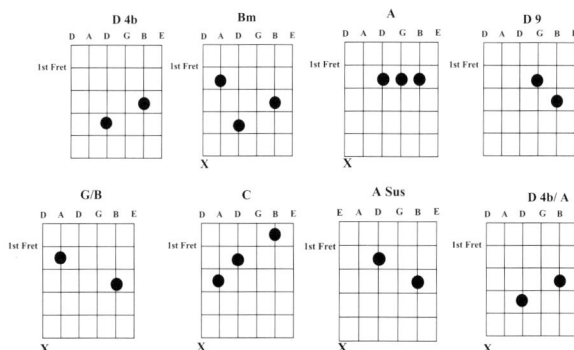

This song uses a dropped D. To do this, tune your bottom E string down to D.

Full moon a-gain [D4] Cast-ing a hue so [Bm] cra [A] — zy [D9]

Mak-ing me blue and [Bm] la — zy [A] Tak-ing eve-ry word to heart [D9] [G|B] [D9]

And when I think I'm do-ing fine [D4] Care-less words can spin [Bm] [A]

Me [D9] Turn-ing a tide with - in [Bm] me [A] Tak-ing me back to the st— [D9] [G|B] [D9]

art Wan-na go to the [C] sea — and let the waves wash o-ver me [C] [Asus] [D4/A]

Need to feel like a [A] [C] child a-gain Smile and then I'u [Bm] [C] [C] [Bm]

stare in-to the [A] eyes [D4/A] of [A] sis-ter moon [D9]

Sister Moon

Chris While and Joe While © Circuit Music

Full moon again
Casting a hue so crazy, making me blue and lazy
Taking every word to heart
And when I think I'm doing fine
Careless words can spin me, turning a tide within me
Taking me back to the start

Chorus
Want to go to the sea and let the waves wash over me
Need to feel like a child again,
Smile and then I'll stare into the eyes of Sister Moon.

Soft light returns
The ovulation's omen, to the womb and the woman
The pull and the pain
And cornered by the field
I am the frost in waiting, to melt in a new day breaking
The wax and the wane

Chorus

The darkness burns
With solitude impending, and darknesses descending
To the very core
Now see the cycle turn
And gone is the pain and sorrow
Bright is the sun tomorrow
Never seen before

Chorus

*My fascination with the sea led me to think about the connections between our environment and us all.
In this case between women and the tides.*

Starting All Over Again

Matthews and While © Circuit Music

Featured on the albums *Piecework* and *Stages*

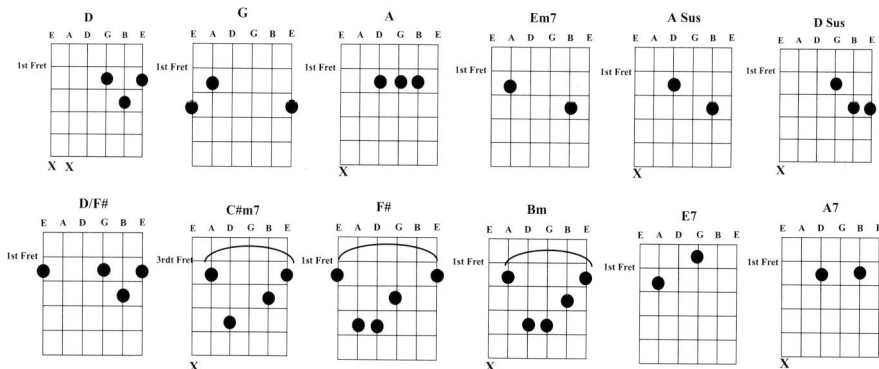

It's a ve-ry long road that's in front of you when you're start-ing all o-ver a-gain You say there's

no way out and there's no way through when you're start-ing all o-ver a-gain And it's

pull-ing in-side of you dimm-ing the light in you Turn-ing your thoughts to yes-ter-day Your

spi-rit is sink-ing low Thoughts have no place to go The tunn-el is clos-ing in a-round you

And it's so hard start-ing all o-ver Start-ing all o-ver a-gain But the

heart finds a way to re-cov-er When you're start-ing all o-ver a-gain

alternative ending

-gain

Starting All Over Again

Matthews and While © Circuit Music

It's a very long road that's in front of you
When you're starting all over again
You say there's no way out and there's no way through
When you're starting all over again
And it's pulling inside of you, dimming the light in you
Turning your thoughts to yesterday
Your spirit is sinking low, thoughts have no place to go
The tunnel is closing in around you

Chorus
And it's so hard starting all over, starting all over again
But the heart finds a way to recover
When you're starting all over again

There's a field of gold under distant skies
Starting all over again
You won't see it till you clear your eyes
Starting all over again
Your heart feels as black as night
It will 'till the time is right
Just for the moment you're holding on
Then turning each corner your heart will grow warmer
And finding your feet you'll be moving forward

Chorus

Your heart feels as black as night, it will till the time is right
Just for the moment you're holding on
Then turning each corner your heart will grow warmer
And finding your feet you'll be moving forward

Chorus x 2

When you're starting all over again

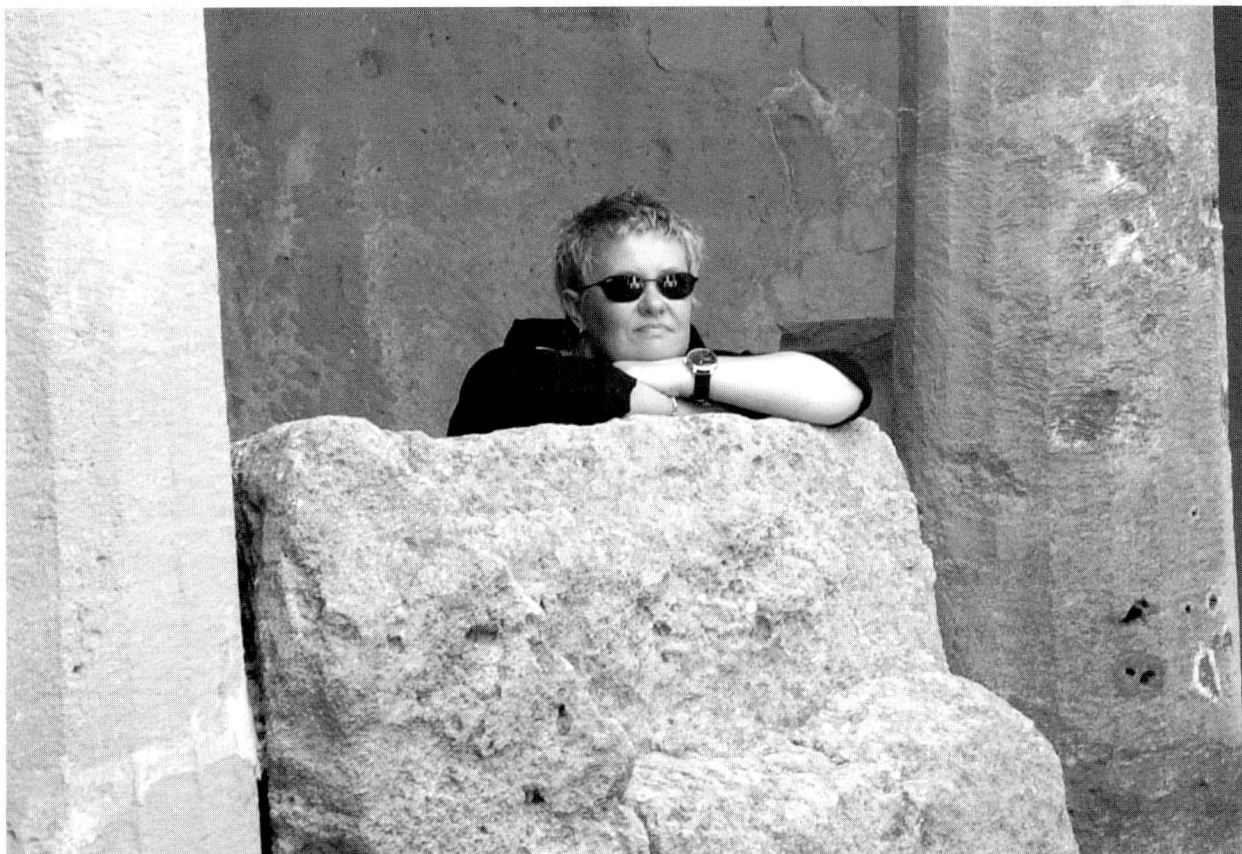

One of our most popular songs. There's always a light at the end of the tunnel, however, it's sometimes hard to see it.

The Devil In Me

Julie Matthews © Circuit Music

Featured on the albums *Such Is Life* and *Stages*

Full moon hot night too tense to sleep too tired to fight

Bad thoughts in my head a ring of fire run-ing round my bed

Well I'm gripped by the fear and the pan-ic of the bott-le Just one taste and I'm

in full thrott-le God have mer-cy keep me from sett-ing free

The de-vil in me

Keep-ing one long step a-head Still-ing the thun-der in my head Cool-ing the

fire in my heart tear-ing and tear-ing a-part

Keep-ing just one drink a-way Keep-ing the ghosts and ghouls at bay Lay-ing to

rest some his-to-ry lett-ing go of the de-vil in me

The Devil In Me

Julie Matthews © Circuit Music

Full moon, hot night
Too tense to sleep, too tired to fight
Bad thoughts in my head
Ring of fire running 'round my head
Well I'm gripped by the fear and the panic of the bottle
Just one taste and I'm in full throttle
God have mercy, keep me from setting free
The Devil in me

Don't want to hurt nobody tonight
But there's somebody else inside me that might
And my mind it's a battlefield
Where the weak ones fall and the strong don't yield
So I pace the floor and I punch out the light
To keep temptation out of my sight
God have mercy, don't let the whole world see
The Devil in me

Chorus
Keeping one long step ahead
Stilling the thunder in my head
Cooling the fire in my heart
Tearing the terror apart
Keeping just one drink away
Keeping the ghosts and ghouls at bay
Laying to rest some history
Letting go of the Devil in me

So God grant me what it takes
To hold tight till the fever breaks
And it will I know this is true
It's just a tunnel I'm crawling through
And I will come out the other side
Wearing my dignity and pride
Oh I can so much stronger be
Than the Devil in me

Chorus (different ending)

Letting go, letting go of
Letting go of the Devil in me

I stopped drinking alcohol when I was 22, it was a life-changing decision, possibly life-saving.
This is the story of the life-long struggle to maintain sobriety.

The Leaving

Matthews and While © Circuit Music

Featured on the albums *Higher Potential* and *Stages*

This song uses a dropped D. To do this, tune your bottom E string down to D.

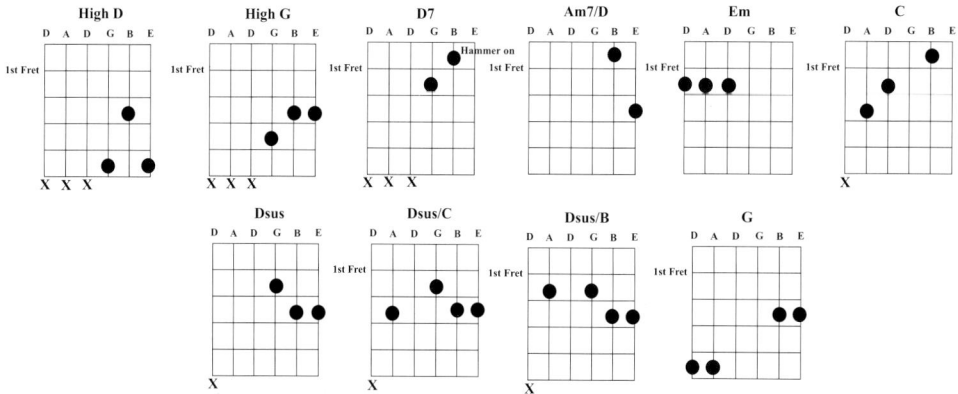

The Leaving

Matthews and While © Circuit Music

There's a well in my heart that is barren and dry now
That echoes the sound of you saying goodbye now
So why the surprise, it was clear in your eyes
Still the weight of your words pin me down like a hand
I'm falling and falling with nowhere to land

Chorus
So I cover my ears – so I can't hear
And I cover my eyes – I don't want to see
'Cause it's over and done bar the leaving

So when you turn don't you dare to look back now
My steely resolve might be tempted to crack now
A crack in the wall, the first tear to fall
Then all of the others come tumbling down
God give me strength if you turn around

Chorus

Don't say a word it might lead to another
Don't look too close you might see through my cover
It's all I can do to see this day through
But how will I feel when I wake up alone
And the ghost of you lingers long after you're gone
And everything's crazy and everything's wrong
And nothing remains of whatever belonged

Chorus

Cover my ears
Cover my eyes
'Cause it's over and done bar the leaving

I think this is the saddest and most heart-wrenching song we've ever written together and it's also one of my favourites. When Chris sings this song live I could cry. The power and emotion gets to me every time.

The Light In You

Julie Matthews © Circuit Music

Featured on the album *Such Is Life*

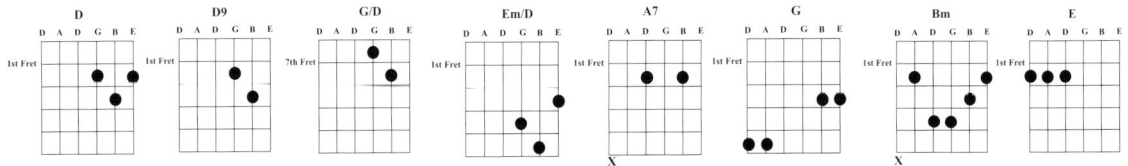

This song uses a dropped D. To do this, tune your bottom E string down to D.

Winds blow me off cen-tre But my aim re-mains ev-er true
I'll foll-ow through the dark-ness I'm gui-ded by the
light in you
Through the long -est dark-est night May I ne-ver lo-
-se your light Love may blind my eyes it's true But my
heart is led by the light in you

The Light In You

Julie Matthews © Circuit Music

Winds blow me off centre
But my aim remains ever true
I'll follow through the darkness
I'm guided by the light in you

Put an ocean in between us
And I'll charter a pathway through
I'll follow through the darkness
I'm guided by the light in you

Through the longest darkest night
May I never lose your light
Love may blind my eyes it's true
But my heart is led by the light in you

Life moves in strange ways but
No shadow will mar my view
I'll follow through the darkness
I'm guided by the light in you

In my heart there burns a fire
You have made the flame grow higher
But nothing burns as bright it's true
As the everlasting light in you

Winds blow me off centre
But my aim remains ever true
I'll follow through the darkness
I'm guided by the light in you

I'll follow through the darkness
I'm guided by the light in you

*Often interpreted as a gospel song, this is simply about a firm belief in someone
– who that someone is, is entirely up to you.*

The Light In My Mother's Eye

Chris While © Circuit Music

Featured on the albums *Higher Potential* and *Stages*

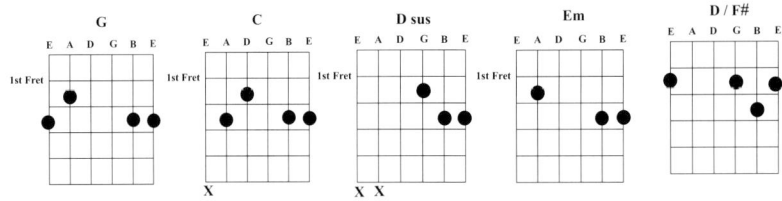

These are the chord shapes we use with the capo on the third fret.

There's a place I can go I'll be wel-come I know Where my child-hood me-mo-ries lie where ans-wers are found Where my feet touch the ground In the light of my mo-ther's eye If she cat-ches my eye my se-crets can't hide no mat-ter how hard I try She knows me best I know I can rest In the light of my mo-ther's eye

The light in my mo-ther's eye —— Still burns in my me-mo-ry as time goes by You can-not re-place the glow on your face From the light in your mo-ther's eye

The Light In My Mother's Eye

Chris While © Circuit Music

There's a place I can go, I'll be welcome I know
Where my childhood memories lie
Where the answers are found –
where my feet touch the ground
In the light in my mother's eye
If she catches my eye, my secrets can't hide
No matter how hard I try
She knows me best I know I can rest
In the light in my mother's eye

Chorus
The light in my mother's eye
Still burns in my memory as time goes by
You cannot replace the glow on your face
From the light in your mother's eye

And who's hand do I take when my heart's set to break
When I'm ready to crumble and cry
Then with courage anew I'll know it was due
To the light in my mother's eye
She will find me some time when she has none
And she helps me to see every side
It's amazing to me the wisdom I see
In the light in my mother's eye

Chorus

When life moved me away, she'd smile and she'd say
There's an unconditional tie
I believe in my heart that you're never apart
From the light in your mother's eye
And at night as I look at my children
And I listen in sleep to their sighs
I hope and I pray they'll see everyday
The light in their mothers' eye

Chorus x 2

*My Mam, Laura, was always a source of inspiration to me. Her generosity and love was never in question.
We could always go to her with any problem and she never judged us. I really miss her still.*

The Thorn Upon The Rose

Julie Matthews © Circuit Music

Featured on the albums *Lies and Alibis*, *Ballads* and *Stages*

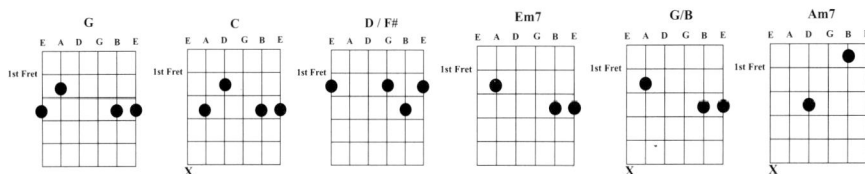

Its taste was sweet like sum-mer wine

The heart that beat in dou-ble time So you waltzed right

in he bowled you o - ver

And you're still reel-ing from the feel-ing when he's gone

The door is closed the lock is turned And

all the pho-to-graphs and lett-ers have been burned So

when you pick the hand-some flow - er

Don't for - get the thorn up-on the rose

Its cut is deep and its scar lasts for-è-ver

It foll-ows love where—ver love goes

The Thorn Upon The Rose

Julie Matthews © Circuit Music

It's taste was sweet, like summer wine
The heart that beat in double time
So you waltzed right in, he bowled you over
And you're still reeling from the feeling when he's gone
The door is closed the lock is turned
And all the photographs and letters have been burned

Chorus
So when you pick the handsome flower
Don't forget the thorn upon the rose
Its cut is deep and its scar lasts forever
It follows love wherever love goes

Just how we fall, it's hard to know
When what we feel we seldom show
So we show the parts we feel are best
And skirt around the edges trying to cover up the rest
You think you know him, he thinks the same
When underneath it all it's just a crazy guessing game

Chorus

Win or lose, it's just the same
Tears of joy or tears of pain
They're hand in hand they come as one
You never meet the moon without the promise of the sun
For all the bruises, for all the blows
I'd rather feel the thorn than to never see the rose

Chorus

It follows love wherever love goes

The simplest songs are often the most popular – this is the most covered of all my songs – notably, Mary Black recorded it on her album 'Babes in the Wood' and subsequently released it as a single. It was also used in a Japanese Television commercial to advertise the 'Silver Bullet' train! I think it's also true that some songs also almost write themselves, the process being unusually easy, that was certainly the case with 'Thorn' it was a gift from my angel.

The Willow

Julie Matthews © Circuit Music

Featured on the album *Intuition*

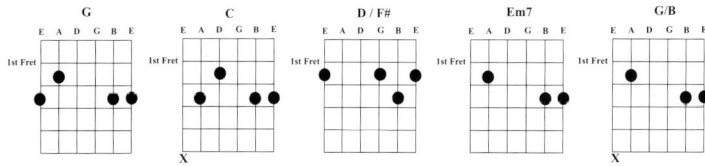

It was un-der-neath the weep-ing will-ow tree
where you swore un-dy-ing love for me How
sweet the prom-ise that could ne-ver be How
sweet the dream we ne-ver came to see I

sat be-neath the will-ow tree and wept For
prom-is-es we made and ne-ver kept A
tear for eve-ry foot-step as you left Be-
neath the will-ow tree I sat and wept

The Willow

Julie Matthews © Circuit Music

It was underneath the weeping willow tree
Where you swore undying love for me
How sweet the promise that could never be
How sweet the dream we never came to see

Chorus
I sat beneath the willow tree and wept
For promises we made and never kept
A tear for every footstep as you left
Beneath the willow tree I sat and wept

Who can know the thoughts and secrets of the heart?
That tears a love to pieces and apart
That leaves a stone where once a flower grew
That turns the world a deeper shade of blue

Chorus

It was underneath our weeping willow tree
She lay within your arms so peacefully
I stood upon the hill and watched you there
You never saw me through her golden hair

Chorus

Beneath our willow tree I sat and wept

This was written specifically for Judy Dunlop to sing on a project called 'Sway With Me'. The only criterion was that there should be some reference to trees. I've always thought the Willow was the most mournful of trees and so it was underneath one that I set the scene for the saddest of stories. It has since been sung and recorded by lots of people including Chris who did an astounding rendition with the Albion Band.

White Water Running

Julie Matthews © Circuit Music

Featured on the albums *Piecework* and *Stages*

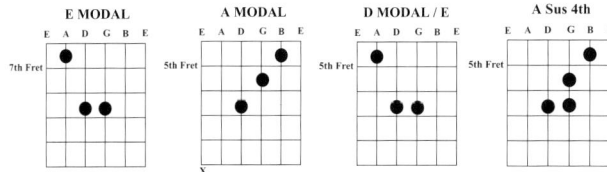

[Emod] I saw it in a dream one night Split the dark like a flash of [Amod] light

[Asus4] Saw my-self in hon-our dress [Amod] With proph-e-cy [Emod] I said I'm blessed

[Emod] I saw a cav-ern in my dreams At the foot of buff-a-lo ra-vine [Amod] And it's

[Asus4] here that I will prove my bra-ve-ry [Amod] It's here that they will [Emod] al-ways speak of me

[Amod] I am white [Asus4] wa-ter [Amod] runn-ing I'm the [Asus4] bra-vest of the [Amod] brave I'm the [Asus4] kee-per of the

[Amod] cave I am white [Asus4] wa-ter [Emod] runn-ing [Amod] I am white [Asus4] wa-ter [Amod] runn-ing one day [Asus4] you will know my

[Amod] name It will [Asus4] ech-o on the [Amod] plain I am white wa-ter [Emod] runn-ing

White Water Running

Julie Matthews © Circuit Music

I saw it in a dream one night, split the dark like a flash of light
I saw myself in honour dress, with prophecy I said I'm blessed

I saw a cavern in my dream, at the foot of Buffalo Ravine
And it's here that I will prove my bravery, it's here that they will always speak of me

Chorus
I am White Water Running, I'm the bravest of the brave, I am the keeper of the cave, I am White Water Running
I am White Water Running, one day you will know my name, it will echo on the plain, I am White Water Running

When the hunters drive the buffalo, many thunder to their deaths below
And I will be the first there at their grave, for I am the keeper of the cave

Chorus

So he found and climbed into his cave, listened for them coming miles away
And White Water Running how he prayed, and the buffalo came, the buffalo came

One by one they fell before his eyes, fifty more before he realised
The keeper of the cave was crushed inside, and along with the buffalo he died

Chorus

On the plains of Alberta stands a small escarpment with an unusual name. Here the Black-foot native Americans used to drive buffalo over the edge to their deaths below. The tribe would then harvest the animals for food, clothing and tools leaving no part of the animal unused. Legend tells of a young Indian brave who hid in a cave at the foot of the escarpment in order to prove his bravery to the rest of the tribe. Unfortunately, so many buffalo came over the edge that they piled up at the bottom and crushed him – hence the name 'Head-Smashed-In Buffalo Jump'

Winter Shines

Chris While © Circuit Music

Featured on the albums *Piecework* and *Stages*

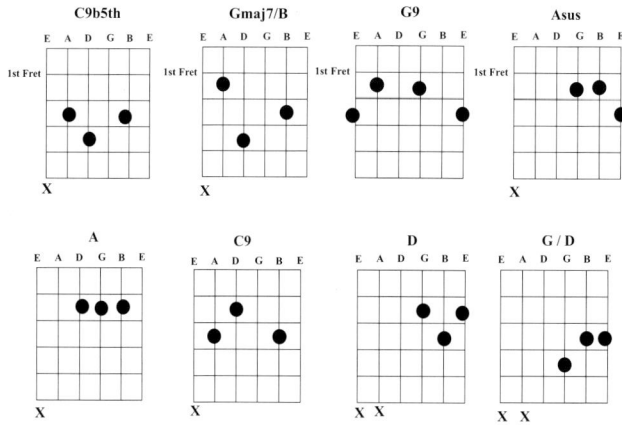

C9b5th Gmaj7/B G9 Asus

A C9 D G/D

[C9b5] It's far from per-fect in this [Gmaj7/B] place though

[C9b5] there's a flower in eve-ry [G9] jar She'll

[C9b5] watch the world through win-dow [Gmaj7/B] lace And

[Asus] count each pass-ing [A] car Once

[D] she could run a-gainst the wind [C9]

[C9] Feel the rain a-gainst her [D] skin But

[G/D] that was spring and now she [D] finds that win-ter [G9] shines

Winter Shines

Chris While © Circuit Music

It's far from perfect in this place
Though there's a flower in every jar
She'll watch the world through window lace
And count each passing car
Once she could run against the wind
Feel the rain against her skin
But that was spring and now she finds
That winter shines

Red roses decorate her walls
Familiar pictures hanging there
And being careful not to fall
She'll find her favourite old blue chair

Once she could run a dozen lives
Watch children grow and say goodbye
But that was summer, now she finds
That winter shines

She reads some letters, writes some too
Then knits and pearls till dinner time
Some faded memories filter though
And through the lace the weather's fine
There was a time when love was warm
A love that weathered every storm
But that was autumn, now she finds
That winter shines

My daughter Kellie and I went to pick my Mam up from a Respite Centre where she had spent a couple of weeks. As we walked in the door we could see her in her wheelchair, handbag in hand, waiting to go home. She beckoned me to come close and whispered in my ear "They all just sit and stare here, they make me feel old and I'm not really". She was 79. It tore my heart out to see them fading. I've used the seasons as metaphors to describe the life span of one woman.

Young Man Cut Down In His Prime

Matthews and While © Circuit Music

Featured on the extended single *Blue Moon On The Rise*

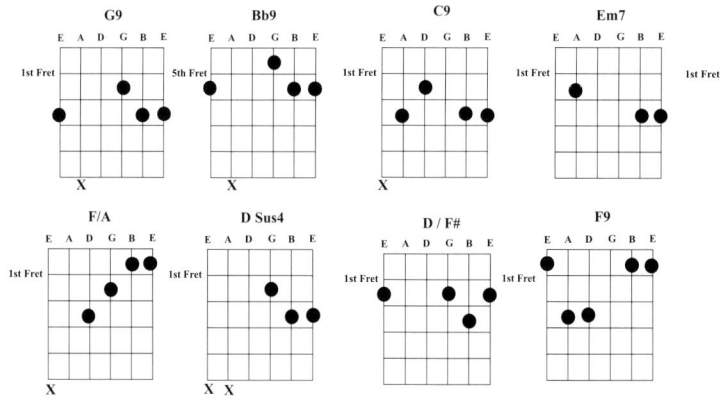

I dreamed a dream of my first born son Es-
[G9] [Bb9] [C9] [G9]

-tranged from me for ten years or more I
[Em7] [F/A] [Bb9] [Dsus] [D/F#]

woke the next mor-ning from tor-ment-ed sleep ——— To
[Em7] [F/A] [Bb9] [G9]

find him weep-ing there at my door
[F9] [C9] [Bb9] [G9]

Last line

I dreamed a dream of my first born son ———
[G9] [Bb9] [C9] [G9]

Young Man Cut Down In His Prime

Matthews and While © Circuit Music

I dreamed a dream of my first born son
Estranged from me for ten years or more
I woke the next morning from tormented sleep
To find him weeping there at my door

Oh Father be not a stranger to me
Open your heart in my hour of need
My body is broken, my time it is near
And I'm trembling under this shadow of fear

This sickness has taken my lover from me
Has taken the life from the friends that were mine
And now I must follow like many before
Oh too many young men cut down in their prime

And when I am dead and they lay me to rest
Ask not for flowers to cover my grave
Ask rather for money to seek and to find
A cure for my brothers so they may be saved

So remember me father with love in your heart
I pray that it blooms with the passage of time
Let love be your healer for love was my crime
And now I'm a young man cut down in my prime

I dreamed a dream of my first born son.

In 1995-96 Roger Watson and Ashley Hutchings launched a scheme called 'The Public Domain'. It was an attempt to encourage writers, both amateur and professional, to carry on the 'word of mouth' tradition of the evolution of songs. Julie and I were part of the birth of this project and our contribution was this song. The original song was 'Young Girl Cut Down in Her Prime'. In the traditional version the girl is stricken with syphilis and is asking her parents for help. In our song the young man has AIDS and is pleading for his estranged father's love and support.

I just LOVE, LOVE, LOVE Chris and Julie's music, they are so full of heart and talent and virtuosity that it fills me with excitement and renewed passion for listening to music.
Kristina Olsen

Chris While and Julie Matthews are performers I could listen to and watch forever. Their singing, songwriting, general musicianship and sheer exuberance and love of life are second to none. Go see them and have your ears blessed - guaranteed to make you come away feeling better about yourself and life in general.
Oh yeah, and they're precious friends as well.
Judy Small

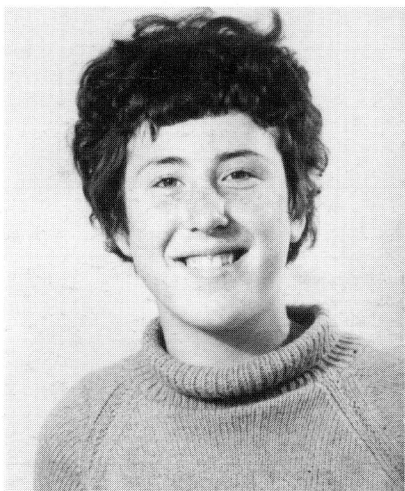

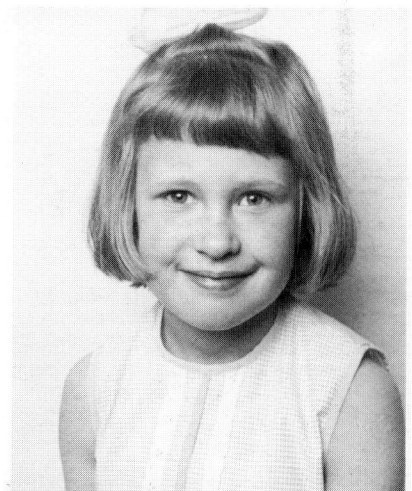